Whisper Unveiled : Verses from the Heart

Somani Baral

BookLeaf Publishing

India | USA | UK

Presentation by *BookLeaf Publishing*

Web: www.bookleafpub.com

E-mail: info@bookleafpub.com

ISBN: 9789360941482

First edition 2024

*For my muse, the love of my life, whose silent
whispers inspired these verses and breathed life
into these pages.*

ACKNOWLEDGEMENT

I am deeply grateful to all those who have contributed to the realisation of this poetry collection, "Whispers Unveiled: Verses from the Heart."

First and foremost, I extend my heartfelt appreciation to my family for their unwavering love, support, and encouragement throughout this journey. Your belief in me has been a guiding light, inspiring me to pursue my passion for poetry. A special mention to my younger sister Pousali who is an important source of motivation and a dedicated critic despite her busy schedule. I am grateful to her for propelling me forward in the moments of doubt.

To my friends and fellow writers, thank you for your invaluable feedback, insightful discussions, and words of encouragement.

I am also indebted to the countless poets and artists whose work has inspired and influenced my own. Your creativity and vision have enriched the world of literature and continue to inspire aspiring writers like myself.

A special thank you to my editor and the
publishing team for the opportunity, their
dedication, expertise, and guidance in bringing
this collection to life.

Last but not least, I express my deepest gratitude
to the readers who have started on this journey
with me. Your support and appreciation for the
written words fuel my passion for poetry and
inspire me to continue sharing my verses with
the world.

Thank you all for being a part of this journey.
May the whispers of the heart continue to
resonate with you long after you turn the final
page.

With heartfelt gratitude,

Dr. Somani Baral

PREFACE

Welcome to the world of poetry, where words dance upon the page and emotions are laid bare. In this collection, I invite you to embark on a journey through the intricate landscapes of the human heart and mind.

Poetry has long been a vessel for expressing the ineffable, capturing fleeting moments of beauty, pain, and everything in between. It is a medium through which we can explore the depths of our own souls and connect with the experiences of others.

As you delve into the verses within these pages, I hope you find solace in the shared human experience, and perhaps glimpse a reflection of your own joys and sorrows. Each poem is a whispered confession, a fragment of truth, a window into the complexities of life.

May these words resonate with you, inspire you, and remind you that you are never alone in the vast expanse of existence. For in the realm of poetry, we are all united by the power of language and the universal yearning to be understood.

Thank you for embarking on this journey with me. Let us explore the depths of the human spirit together, one verse at a time.

A letter of Reflection and Reminder

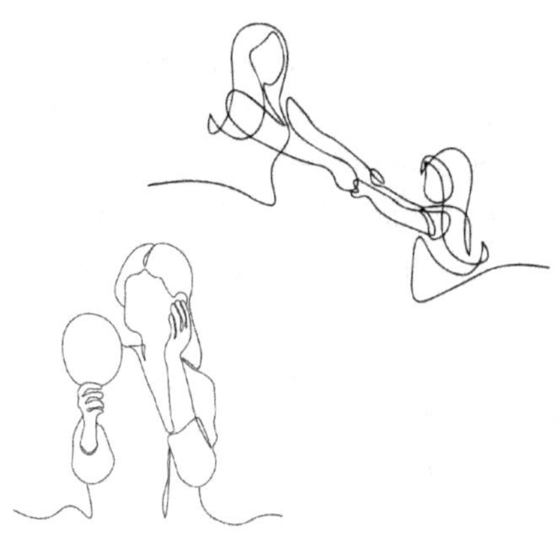

Dear Younger Me,
First of all congratulations on being an adult.
Official freedom awaits you.

Mirror which saw you in stethoscope,
And an apron with a beautiful smile,
Congratulations, you will become a doctor.
The famous college life,
You're going to experience it.

First anatomy dissection class to practical vivas.
First success to first failure,
First friendship to first fight,
First love to first heartbreak,

Mirror will see you in all your faces,
Sometimes with a beautiful smile;
Sometimes glowing with elegance;
Sometimes dark circles over sleepless nights;
Sometimes pain hidden in glees;
Sometimes tears veiled in drops of rain;
Nevertheless, all will be cherished memories to
cheer for.

Remember you are strong,
You are beautiful,
You are enough;
Because you are the steering wheel of your life.
But I have something to tell you;
You will think it's all over.
You will be completely broken,
But guess what,
Hold on and take a deep breath.
A day will come,
When you will be at the centre stage
And the mirror will witness the different you.
That day you will know, wanting to be
Someone else is a waste of what you are,
So be you.

But you will still focus on your negatives.
Because people have conditioned you to look a
certain way,
Demoralised you will stop seeing dreams.
But should I tell you this,
The dreams you loved will make you do things
you never thought you could.

Spoiler alert,
Life has crazy plans for you,
Because you don't know it,
people will tell you,
You are not good enough,
Forget all that craziness and compromise with it.

Please!
Never stop believing your ways,
Your dreams and struggles for me.
Your hobbies will be yours.
And you will love them.

You are the only one and you walk alone;
Listen to the music of your heart,
Lately when you look in the mirror,
You will know,
What you were, what you are,
What you will become.

Believe in yourself and you will achieve your
dream.
Loving Future Me.

A Visual Odyssey

Holding pixels in my hand,
Telling stories inscribed in the cells of my heart,
Unscripted moments perfectly captured,
Those witnessed by the sands of time.
Innocent smiles,
Spirits of childhood,
First day of school,
To every first time,
Clicks of each milestone achieved,
Celebrating those moments of joy.

Snapped, clicked, captured;
Unveiling beautiful chapters,
Moments that stood out in the gallery for the
best.

We sat together,
Articulating silent stories,
Breathing life into the timeless narrative
That the picture holds,
Provoking giggles and guffaws.
Now the funny moments captured
Forming an aura of laughter,
While reviving moments of togetherness.

Visual diary of growing up,
As squad shines,
Memories thrive,
Friendship framed.
Nostalgia in every detail
Ageing like fine pixels.

Selfies to serve self,
Or circles of companions,
Sweet smiles and cute styles,
Illuminating emotions with the click of the
shutter,
The beauty of yesteryears,
Embracing imperfections over time.

Dusting off the pixels of the past,
As time travels,
But nothing changes the adorable vibes.
Rather eternal imprints left behind,
For generations to unravel.

Walking through time with visual tales.
One snapshot resonating vibes timeless,
Together all converge,
In those ephemeral moments,
To embark on a journey,
Uniquely mine,
With us together.

Shades of Love

Love is pure
When a newborn smiles, staring at the mother.
Love is prayer
When you have faith in the universe.
Love is perseverance
When you don't give up despite difficulties.
Love is protection
When siblings stand up for you, against anyone
who hurts you.
Love is power
When it heals you.

Love is freedom
When you let your wings fly high.
Love manifests as kindness
When it offers help unconditionally.
Love abounds
When nature fulfils all the essentials for
survival.
Love is that brightness

Which brings sunshine to the caved dark lives.
Love is a music
Tuning the connection of hearts.

Love is friendship
When you share unfiltered feelings with your
bestie.
Love is that bond when two unknown people
sign forever.
Love is beyond boundaries and barriers.
Love is the strength to fight against all odds and
the trust that brings us all together.
Love is never boastful but sparkles in the eye
that beholds.
Love is a language that doesn't need a translator.
Love is the shade that imbues our world with
joy, happiness and prosperity.

Tales of Two

Walking down the memory lane,
Through tears and laughter,
Recalling moments, so fine.

Amidst the anguish,
Seeking the warmth of mother's lap,
Through tears, blurring everything around;
As emotions swayed,
Catching a glance into her dark brown eyes,
Her skin fair as snow,
And slowly grasping her hands, so soft and tiny.

They said, "She's your cute little sister."
An innocent heart understood nothing,
But found a pal to play with.
In my tender small arms, held her close;
Sometimes stumbling
In my own newfound steps.

Time flew, as we grew;
Swinging our hands to school,
In books, knowledge entwined;
Dancing in the rain,
To the summer vacay.
Each holiday a secret silver screen time to play.

Fun to fight,
In the tussle of love's affection, we vied.
In the battle of love, bond did grow.
In the depth of silence, emotions resided,
Few unspoken tales, within our hearts
We did hide,
Until that day.

At three in the morning, heard the clock's soft
chime,
Yet conversation flowed, like the sweetest
rhyme,
In the stillness of the night, words took flight,
Boundless as stars in the velvet night.

Time's steady march, in silence abate,
As souls connected, in the hour late.

In the dawn of friendship, a bond anew,
Beyond sisterly shields, our hearts pursued.
Feelings unfiltered,
Secrets disclosed,
And pages turned open,
Respecting priorities in trust's embrace.

Two sisters, one coin's gleaming sheen,
Each other's puzzle, unveiled and keen,
In solace found, problems fade away,
Pillars of strength, come what may.

Sometimes words unspoken, understood in
silence,
Bound by threads of love,
Together we soar in skies untold,
As our hearts forever intertwine.

To my Mother

Many splendoured miracles
Like mysteries of creation,
One of God's tender guiding hand,
My first home on Earth,
Is the water of her Womb.
She pulled herself in pain,
To welcome me to the world.

Her Love, so pure and eternal.
She gave her heart,
when mine felt apart.
She gave her eyes
To see the best in the worst.
She gave her spirit,
To help me grow anew.
She kissed to wipe my tears,
And a warm hug to ease my fears.
She directed my passion
To which I was unaware.

She is the well-wisher
For all my success.

Distance could never do us apart.
In my silence, she knew my pain;
In my cry, she knew my hunger;
In my smile, she knew my feelings;
A best friend in disguise,
May the whole world be busy otherwise.

The epitome of deep devotion
Of sacrifice and pain.
It's endless and selfless,
Her love is patient and forgiving.

She is my pillar of strength to face
the challenges with confidence,
Moreover wisdom to choose the battle wisely.

She gave the greatest gift of life to me,
Taught to love,
And be kind
But strong as well as resilient.
Then in love, she set me free.

I hope when you think of me,
You'll see a part of you,
As I wish to make you proud Mother.

Forever Father's Princess

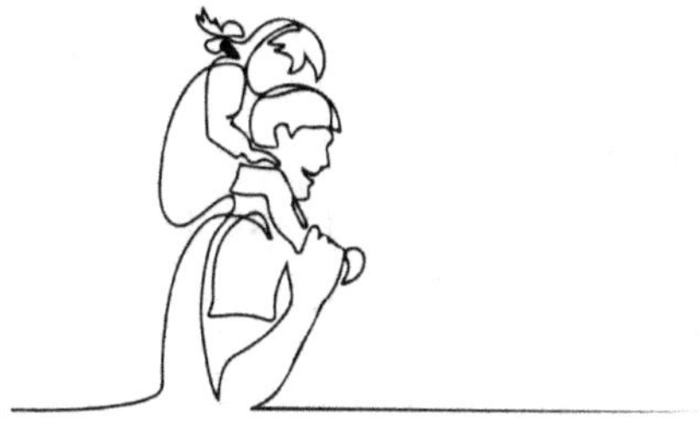

As I walk through the aisle,
Ready for the wedding vows,
I see tears welling up in his eyes.
Flashbacks hit us,
From holding his hand
On the first day of school,
To the first day of hostel life.
I remember every fall,
Sometimes from a bicycle,
Sometimes in exams,
Sometimes in life,
To be held up by his big arms.

A Father's love is unique and beautiful,
Stubborn and strict,
But tender like a coconut.

He taught me how to stand and fight,
To grow independent,
Be it in my career,
Or in my personal life,
Be it in success,
Or in failure.

A determined heart,
Sacrificed hours to build my future,
Struggles notwithstanding,
Fulfilling all my dreams.
A proud heart,
Even in my smallest achievements,
Celebrating with gifts and joy.

In my little cries, his heart sobs;
And there he is with buckets of ice cream.
In my silence, his mind thinks a thousand
thoughts;
In my future, he has planned several foresights.
In my struggles, he paves the way with flowers,
so bright.

I could hold his head high,
Is what I am proud of.
Before I am my husband's queen,
I will forever be my father's princess.

Of friends who always

I am surrounded by friends,
Who knows how to love.
Be it, when I was a little girl
Or as women,
Within the rules of society braided in my curls,
They gave me lessons in empathy.
Beyond the syllabus of sciences,
As we study the anatomy of each other's hearts.

My friend taught me to smile through
adversities.
Wrapped in bond,
Beyond bands and cards.
Till the day I knew its meaning,
Friendship became as sacred as love,
Deeper than words.

Through secrets researched and gossips shared,
Through every failure and heartbreak,
Holding each other's hand.
Through every silly joke,
Heart held lighter,
Laughter held loud.
Through emotional commitment,
To be understood and you understand.

No questions,
And no judgments,
Unfiltered feelings fill in the gap.
My guardian way from home,
When I return late.
My alibi when bumpers hit my path.

They know all my flaws and disguises.
Recognising my mood swings,
And aware of every phase.
They are like my antennae,
Reading through minor inconveniences to major
crises.

There's no proof and receipt to be enough,
As they celebrate our joy prouder than us,
Standing hand in hand,
Shielding against malicious stares.
They build a safe space

Outside corridor
In the house of our own.

Of friends who always
Open their mind,
Free their schedule to listen to us.
Every time we stumble,
Drunken or drained in laughter,
Faint whisper heard
"It's alright, it has to be."

Days go by,
Still, we sing our favourite friendship song.
Dancing in madness,
In the prophecy of love,
And politics of hatred.
We created a safe shared path,
Within our insecurities,
To follow each other's story till deep ends.

Behind every successful person
There are also buddies who bind.
For centuries, through arts and poetry,
We're overwhelmed by love,
To which I don't disagree,
But friendship is no less a synonym.

A Summer Bliss by the Shore

Begins summer on the beach,
Scorching heat
Under beach umbrellas,
Kissed by the sun;
Quenching thirst,
As we sip
Watermelon and Mango,
Juicy and sweet
Savouring each bite.

Summer's laughter and fun,
Frolicking on the sand,
A picnic on the dune,
As we play volley.
Leaping and diving,
Splashing water on each other,

Cheers and shouts echoes,
Mingling with the tide.

Amidst the rustle of the palm trees,
With ocean breeze in the air,
We find ourselves,
Sometimes lounging with a novel,
Or sunbathing on the warm sand.

Salt and sand combined,
As footprints trace our laughter,
Moments drift like shells upon the shore,
Summer's bliss, we couldn't ask for more.

Portrait of a Lady

"Come 'ere my dear," she whispered, soft and
slow.
As she saw me from far,
Emotions rolled down in tears as I came near.
Those wrinkled hands that once knew grace,
Now tremble as they cup my face.
Fortunate to have her blessings and love, so
dear.

Years gone by,
Weathered not her soul.
Wisdom gathered passed over generations.
With silvery hair,
Gentle eyes but a little blurred,

In a cosy chair by the hearth's warm glow,
With garbled speech,
She uttered,
"Believe, life's a beautiful journey."

Echoed laughter, tears and praise.
Her love a shelter, strong as walls,
Through murmurs and mumbles.
Truth still shines
In every phrase
Carrying a message, timeless.

Still, I remember those,
Tender soft memories of lullabies, so clear.
Special sweet treats in festive,
Nourishing delicacy to hearty meals,
Preserves from summer's lavish yield,
Nurtured in her fertile field.

From knitting sweaters in winter
To her art and craft, a timeless lore,
Legacy through her diverse talent.
As she shapes the clay, each sculpture tells a
tale.

Sometimes beads,
Sometimes silent hymns of prayer,
Sage timeworn weaves her love into every heart,
Grandma's touch, eternal and divine.

A Nostalgic Reverie

Underneath my outside face,
There's a face none can see.
A little less hard,
A little more child,
But a whole lot more like me.

Downhill I go,
Hopping through streets of chocolates,
Dancing in the rain,
Or drawing houses in the sand,
As summer holidays, a blissful retreat,
Brings days of sunshine, laughter and play.

Sometimes counting stars in the sky so high,
On full moon nights, under its gentle sigh,

Wishing upon shooting stars,
To share secrets with the night.
As planes soar high, dreams take flight,
And reminisce unfurl.

Revisiting moments,
In time's gentle pace,
Through the corridor of yesterday's grace,
Each memory, a treasured place,
In innocent acts and plays that we shared.

Nostalgia of inner innocence.
From hugging my favourite doll,
To sketching art of fascination,
Moreover, the cries over innocent demands,
Or stealing sweets in festive hue,
All are clear memories, so dear.

Childhood, an imaginative world full of new
experiences:
Watching cartoons,
As Bob the Builder builds childhood,
Or Shaktiman teaching morals,
Harry Potter stickers on notebooks,
Rolling sixes in Ludo,
Or winning a full house of Cards,
And crying over falling down in Snakes and
Ladders.

Entering school,
Memories bloomed,
Through laughter and fun,
Mischief with friends, a fond adieu.
Playing hide and seek in bunches.
Sharing and stealing tiffin,
From fighting over silly things,
Yet hearts entwine.
To reach the finish line of a cheerful childhood.

Uphill I go,
When time gives way to months and years,
The door opens to adolescence.
Crushing over the movie star's bright blaze,
Caught in whispering gossip's maze.
Mature mind swings between tide of transition,
And complexities of emotions.
As the age trespasses,
Bold and beautiful feelings rise,
In the tide of change, love defies.

In the flow of time's motion,
I delve deep,
Seeking back the notion,
To find the treasure,
The pebbles of innocence once again,
And throw it into the ocean of childhood.

Symphony of Like and Love

The clock clicks at 3 a.m.
A confused mind
And bare awake eyes felt,
The music of a bounding heart.
As like and love entwine,
Two souls converge
To a symphony Divine.

As the chapters of memoir unfold,
Smile grace the blushed cheeks,
Like the alchemy of hearts,
Love breaks all notions,
To encapsulate eternal emotions.

Like the gentle breeze,
Whisper soft and mild.
Or love's fierce flame,
Passionate and wild.

Like the morning dew on a rose bloom,
Or love's enduring light vanishes gloom.
Like the pages of the book worn and old,
Or Love's story holding a treasure untold.

Like the feather's touch, light and airy;
Or Love's embrace, warm and merry.
Like the river's flow, steady and serene;
Or Love's tidal wave, an invincible desire.

Like the star above, distant and shiny;
Or Love's constellation creating destiny.
Like the horizon where hope takes flight,
Or Love's possibility promises forever delight.

Like the artist's stroke subtle and exquisite;
Or Love's masterpiece, a priceless infinite.
Like the woven threads in a fine tapestry,
Or Love's moment stitched with care
Creating memories of mastery.

In the realm of emotions,
Both like and love intertwine,
To cherish the gift divine,
And harmonies blend in a melody, sublime.

The Bare branch and Beach

Stand still the bare branch
And empty bench
To witness
Sometimes the waves kissing the shores,
Or sunbathing weary souls,
Sometimes eyes gazing at the sparkling star in
the moonlight.
Or sheltering birds twittering to tune of the tide.

Bare stand the branch
To hold the lagoon,

A spot hiding mysterious sea life,
And beautiful shades of blue water.
The love buds blooming there,
Bound to the music of their hearts.

The bare branch buried are
Signs of sea life,
Following shadow in the sand of the beach,
Flows the seashells with pearl in it,
While sand dunes guarding the shore,
Sights of which are majestic mysteries.

The bare branch and beach,
Oblivious to all the chaos.
The Ethereal beauty,
And unbound love,
Complimenting the flow,
And capturing the unfathomable depth of
connection.
Bold and firmly rooted,
Stand still the bare branch in the sand of time.

Love at First Sight!!

No it won't be love at first sight,
when we meet,
It'll be love at first remembrance,
Because I've seen you in my mother's eyes
when she tells me to marry the type of man,
She would want to raise her son to be like.
Because I've seen in you the reflection of my
Father so ideal,
While manifesting the love my parents share
Within both happiness and hardship.

No it won't be situationship
As the generation today shares.
It'll be love, forever and infinite.
As we hold hands of friendship,
Growing old as permanent partners.

No it won't be love at first sight,
When we meet,
It will be a moment so dear.
'Cause I will have seen you in our daughter's
eyes,
When she tells her father to be her prince
charming.

No it may be late to be your first love,
But never late to do anything to be your last.
Because I have seen you in God's plan,
And in the conspiracy of the universe.
When I received better than what I prayed for.

Always You

At five in the morning's hush,
All my friends talk about that night, I flush.
Remembering the pledge,
Bold decision made at the edge.
"Never going to fall in love,"
Knowing that it's either Heart or Mind.

Close to surrender, on the brink I stood,
Then you arrived in my daydreams,
that I saw.
Pinch me, for I'm lost in this reverie,
Unbelievable, your presence, this reality.
In and out, I sway for you;
Defying norms, breaking through.

Love, an unexpected prize,
You nestled in to my surprise.
Not to love, I vowed before your name,

I claimed,
Yet hopeful, I hold, you'll feel the same.
Confiding secrets none else encloses,
You, earthly heaven, my heart's repose.
"No," I have never been the one,
So cliché, but it's true.

Falling for you way too often,
In melodies of our song sung,
In moments, dancing when no eyes are strung,
You got all my days and nights,
No regrets, not even echoes of our past,
Discovering now the patience that lasts.
Holding a mirror to my soul's embrace,
Learning to reflect, in wisdom's grace.

All I do is think about you.
Your leap of faith, guides my own;
In your trust, my belief finds its due,
Letting you go would be a sin,
As love doesn't come around all the time.

Broken heart ain't hard to find,
Grateful you possess mine,
In joy's bright glow or depths of despair,
Know, in every high or low,
You're never alone, in sorrow's tide,
In pieces, I'll stand by your side.
Through every fall, in love's maze,

Forever present, in endless ways.

Life's path, a winding road unknown,
In silence, I dwell,
How to express thee?
But there's beauty in chaos,
Awaiting fate's decree,
In the ebb and flow of life's grand sea
You'll find me there,
For it's always thee.

The Proposal Prescription

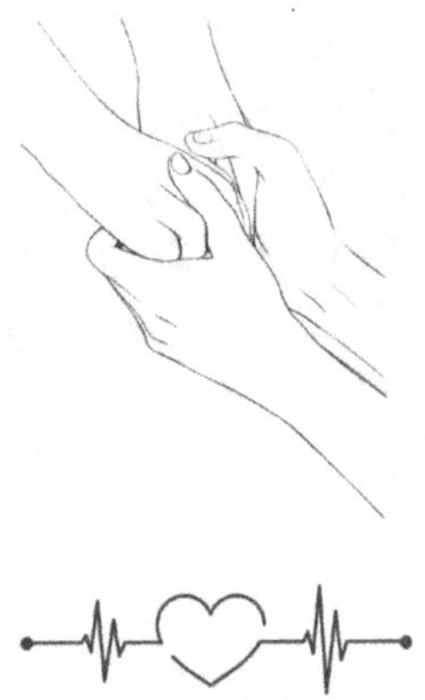

In tomes of Medicine, as pages unfolded.
You came in like a whisper, gentle and bold.
Hormone of my happiness.
Glucose for my hypoglycaemia.
Alleviated my aches,
As a delight to my reward centre.

An unknown feeling did flush my blushing face,
A kaleidoscope of emotion, in a fleeting chase.
Nerves carried a network, etched in the heart.
Cheeks never stopped smiling,
Eyes never stopped gazing.
Through the labyrinth of feelings, they roam,
Raising my serotonin levels.

As sight of you jumbled my biochemical
reactions,
My hormone levels reported
"You are in love dear."
ECHO echoed love.
Brain knew no emotion except love.

Head over your shoulder is a pleasure of mine.
Hugging you is a relaxation to all my worries;
Hours of staring, weary eyes find reprieve;
In your touch, trembling hands believe;
Voices of your verses soothe my ears.
Dumb to the chaos of blabbers.
Dancing to the tune of our hearts.

Anxieties, like tempests, churned within.
Fibrillatory waves racing, where fears begin.
Yet trust and faith, a balm serene;
Palliated pain and breathlessness unseen.

Captured in my mind are fond memories of us.
Connecting waves of beat,
Stay forever in the muscle memory of our hearts.
Destiny of our destination is you.
To the invisible plexus of nerve connecting us,
I want you to be mine forever, infinitely.

Dew drops on A Rose

In the dawn's tender light,
As it rained,
A rose stands tall.
On its velvet lips,
Dewdrops rest,
Shining like a diamond,
Poised by tiny jewels.

Each drop a crystal, pure and bright,
Reflecting the world in its fragile sphere.
Nature's tears in the hush of night,
Whispering secrets only rose hears.

Dewdrops like a glistening pearl,
In the sun's first light,
Blushed the crimson petal,
Capturing the essence,

Where dreams are newly born,
Fleeting romance in nature's glance.

The rose awakens, bathed in gleam,
A silent witness to the night's gentle tear.
Dewdrops vanish in the morning light,
But their ephemeral beauty, forever bright.

Cup of Purple Tea

I didn't know those violet leaves,
sprinkled over green could make purple tea,
Prettiest and tastiest.

But he made it for me,
When I asked for a cup of lemon tea,
Oh no!!
It's already late in the evening,
Closed are shops after shops,
Will the lemons be available?
Lucky he got what he wanted,
Yes!! Flattered, it's for me.

He made it after a long time.
And ten little leaves of violet,
Smiled down from the jar
Brewing into the boiling water.

Our eyes turned to tea,
As blue turned purple tea.

My favourite part was squeezing the lemon
juice.
Surprise and delighted me,
Felt like holding his hand
And kissing.
As we sip down a cup of purple tea,
Is it too hot, or is it just him?
I felt nothing amidst the soothing sight before
me.

As he continues to sip through his brown lips,
carefree.
Frenzied emotions swirl within,
Like today and yesterday,
And the day before that,
Maybe some days after that.

In the here and now,
As we spoke,
Words slipped away,
Lips touched,
And I forgot what I was going to say next,
Flowing into the moment, so romantic.

From My Heart to Your Eyes.

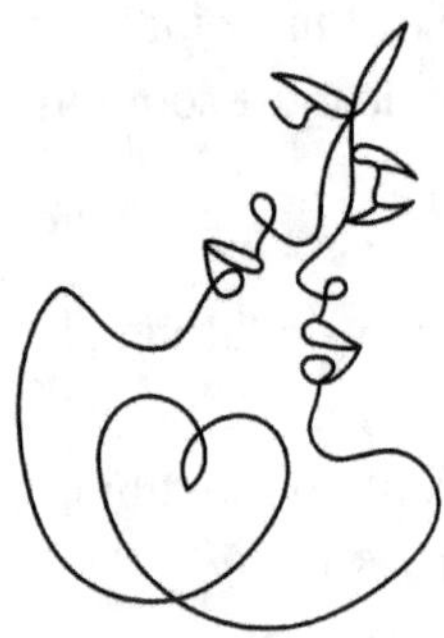

Last night for the first time,
O' heart's delight,
In the night's show of milky lights,
O' those beautiful bubbly eyes,
Skipped a beat of my heart.

All was black and dark,
Glimmering the northern lights;
In the north, alone
In the moment of our own.

Eyes spoke
The unspoken silence,
With calm and stillness in the background,
As all shone in its brilliance.

Under open skies as our playground,
O' in that blue suit,
Like the flying butterfly in the eternal garden,
Began fluttering in my heart.

Through your eyes,
Heart can never lie.
Dearest moment our souls beheld,
And loved you at first sight.

Etched in my Heart,
Is a piece of angelic art,
As my thirsty pen sketches,
O' bliss to my benevolent eyes.

The golden sun with warming tides,
Now the ocean where we dance besides.
To tunes of heart rejoicing,
Like the happy birdie singing.

Sight of your glance,
I am in your trance,
Secret treasure hidden
As I see through the eyes of your heart.

Closed eyes dreaming,
Countless ways,
Holding my heart captive, it will never stray,
As the sun rises and darkness becomes day.

Your precious heart,
Held in my gentle hands,
To the belief,
Placed in God's plan.

Coffee Date!!

In the famed coffee shop,
That timeless, cherished spot,
Where old flavours linger,
Romantic novel cradled in my hand,
Love stories gently unfolded—
Isn't it so lovely?

As raindrops dance on windows,
Water drips from a closed umbrella,
Time begins to slow,
In this cosy, wistful haven,
Where do all true lovers go?

Sometimes imagining,
Sometimes blushing,
As I read through those lines,
That bloom, when eyes first meet,
And you find yourself entangled in his words,
First touch, hearts anew.

And then one day,
You start to feel the heaviness of losing him,
But each had its unique twists.
Lessons learnt as chapters unfurled,
It's never over till it's actually over.

Madam, your coffee!!
Yes, a heart etched on it,
Each sip a sweet connection,
In a world of tales retold.
While the pages whispered the secret of hearts,
Both brave and bold.

With each sip, I delve deeper
Lost in realms of my reverie.
As caffeine courses through my veins,
Engrossed in thoughts so fine.

There, I sketch his smile;
Cute dimple dancing in his stubble beard,
Brown lips gently curved,
Small dark eyes,

With blackish-brown wavy hair.

There, I scribble more;
To ink down tale of two unknown souls,
For the generation ahead.
It's rain and coffee,
Canvassing my mind,
Nevertheless, a romantic date.

Birdie and Chicky

Chicky said he will dance with the kid,
If she can sing the song of joy;
Inside the cage, hanging,
From the roof of the porch.
Little Birdie looked through the bars and
wondered,
"On what little things happiness depends,"
Looking into his innocent eyes.

Birdie tweeting in the morning,
While Chicky starts clucking,

She rises to give the morning alarm to the early
riser,
Then they both set the rhythm of their day.

Little Birdie loves her home,
And all the creatures in and around it.
Morning after morning she sang,
Little did she know him.
Told her story to the stars,
And to people passing by.

Small eyes, brown body
Perched on his featherless leg,
Hopping through the fences,
He played with kids.
Sight of him appeases her eyes,
And soothes her voice.
Days went by,
She in her cage,
Freed her heart,
"Here, at last, feelings of strange longing."

Love is a wonderful thing,
More precious than the emeralds.
It's priceless, nor can it weigh out in balance for
gold.
Her love dancing to the sound of her music,
While butterflies flutter around to celebrate love.

She purred to Chicky, dear and divine.
"In every verse of mine, you do shine."
"Nay, it cannot be, our worlds don't align,
Yours soaring high, while mine's a world of
trade and conquest,"
Said he.

Little she could say,
"You are my world, my highs and lows."
With a bold heart, Chicky ventured far and free,
Though it wasn't easy for him either.
Days passed by with no sign of him,
As the flock was chosen, and bound for the
fields far away.

Beneath the moonlit sky, she bowed in love's
embrace,
For her beloved, she sang, each note a tender
swoon,
Lovers danced to her tune.

'Be happy, Be happy," cried the nightingale,
"You shall have what is yours."
"There's a way," whispered the Tree.
"Spread the wings and sing melodies where the
horizon lies."

Birdie felt a glimmer of hope and sang with
grace,

To the Master's joy offered release,
But she chose to be.
In her heart, she found her wings.
She continued to sing
Pouring her love and her life into the music.

Up in the heaven, the Eagle God watched,
He asked, "Why persist Little Bird undaunted?"
Little Birdie replied, "It's nature's unique
wonder,
To inspire belief.
If I give up, people will lose faith in love,
And won't trust in heaven's gift."
Blessed by the Eagle God's might,
Little Birdie soared,
Love's beacon of light.

Yet love's potent pull held sway,
Till one fine morning,
Her sweet song, he did hear.
He returned at last, drawn by love's gentle call.

A miracle of love, in their gaze, it shone clear,
As Chicky leaps to have sight of his Little
Birdie.
Bounding with joy,
Their reunion, a sight divine,
Their eyes sparkled with love.
In the power of love, differences fade away,

Come what may.
With the sunrise, they rise to sing,
Awakening the world,
To start new beginnings.

Wish master

It's 12 on the clock,
Wished my mind with eyes closed,
Cold breeze passing through the shivering body,
Walking through the dark path,
Whispering the still tree,
On watching my blushed face.

Flashbacks hit me when our eyes met first
But what exactly is love?
Love is felt not defined,
Love is patience,
Love is not holding onto but letting go.

If I could call him mine;
If silence was not fluttering our hearts,
If only chords hit the right string
And sing the music of our love.

To have a sight of him is what my eyes yearn
for,
To hear a voice of him is what my ears tune to,
To have a hug is what my heart bounds to,
To have a kiss is what my lips sense,
To have his hand in my hand always and forever.

Smile on his face is a pleasure of mine.
One day his heart will hit mine,
To join the fragments of incompleteness;
To the rays of belief from heaven that brought us
together,
Definitely, maybe.

Things I couldn't say

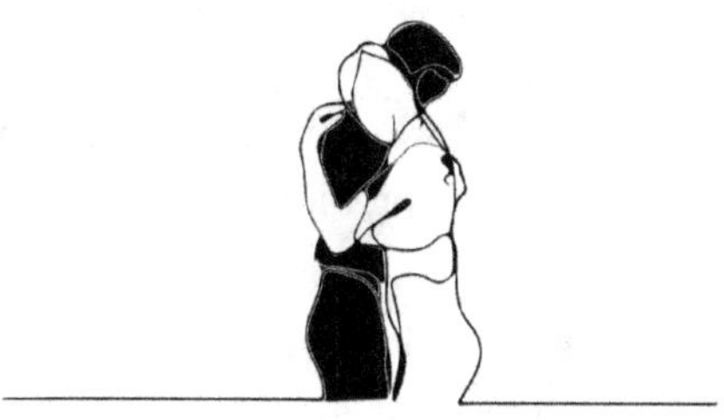

I wrote and erased,
Again and again,
O' this love
Feel thou perplexed
How do I say this?
Again!

When I said just for tonight,
I meant to be with you forever.
When I said hate me,
I meant to love me indefinitely.
When I said I was upset with you,
I meant to never give up on you.
When I opened up, my heart laid bare,
I meant to trust you beyond comparison.
When I urge you not to leave,
I meant I feared losing you.

I crave for you in my days and nights,
I yearn to say goodnight and give forehead
kisses,
And to say I adore you when you feel at your
worst.
I long for you in ways where I just want to be
next to you and nothing more or less.

Behind each glance, a story,
Each smile, a hidden plea,
As days passed by
Learnt to love more,
Felt free and freed,
For the love I have for you,
To love myself.

The Freed Cage

A bird confined, in a cage's bars ensnared,
Its spirit, undeterred, to the world declared.
She stalks down the narrow cage,
Can seldom see through her bar of rage.
With clipped wings, she strives to flee,
But freedom's call remains a distant echo.

Caged Bird sings with fearful thrill,
Of things unknown but longed for still.
Grounded by fear of loss,
Bound by limit, a heavy cross;
As wings grow weak, she can't ascend;
In shadows of doubt, she finds no end.
Feather takes a longer to regrow,
Diminished flesh loses its glow,
Can the imprisoned soul still find its way?

Then came one to set her soul alight,
With love's tender touch.

Together they sang, their hearts in clutch.
Nurtured her inner strength,
Her value unearthed.
"Fly high, proclaim your worth,
Sing, Free Bird;
Letting your voice resound,
To the world's ear,
May your love be found."

And there she stands,
The free bird,
Waiting for another breeze.
This time her tune heard
From the distant hill,
For the caged Bird sings of freedom.
She reached the sky soaring high,
As wings of liberty released her inner tie.

In the power of confidence and trust,
Releasing from the grip of caged emotions'
might,
The fence no longer captivated her in its plight.
Within the confines, she discovers her own,
A universe inside where she has grown.

I know but I don't know

I know you know what you should know.
It's interesting!!
How soul can be within our body,
But out of reach sometimes.

You think the way it shouldn't be interpreted.
You feel like you're defeated before the battle
even begins.
You feel restless when you need to be patient.
You feel lost in the turbulence of life.
You feel misunderstood before you could even
explain.

You feel scared of the future, unknown.
You feel guilty for not turning up as expected.
You look where there is nothing to seek.
You get touched unto the moment you have the
least control.
Words spoken go unheard in the voices heard.

We often surrender control of our thoughts,
Giving others power over us.
We expect things to go a certain way.
We let ourselves defined by the metric of
normal,
The norms set by society,
"Right" or "Wrong".

But I also know,
No problem is greater than ourselves.
When we choose
Happiness in despair,
Believe in lost hopes,
Faith in Supreme touch.
When we choose to redefine the unknown
known.

Heart Owned

In the quiet of the evening,
When the stars begin to gleam,
I find my thoughts returning,
To a tender, wistful dream.

My heart, once free and wandering,
Now owned by love so true.
Every beat and every whisper,
Belongs to only you,
Which I came to know too late.

Sometimes love drives you crazy,
Like a restless heart in sheer delight.
And I run like road rash,
Just to catch a glimpse of his face in sight.

Yet love's tales are seldom smooth,
Twists and turns in every lore,
When commitment falters,

Bound by chains,
Of status, society, and more.

Then time, the miles, the battles fought,
Test the strength of hearts entwined,
As they stumble, rise and fall.

Love is free,
His choice I respect.
Voices urge to move on, to let love wane,
Yet from inside, I choose to stay.

As seasons pass,
And months take flight.
In the race of time,
I hold steadfast, in my own rhyme;
Away from the chaos outside.

Sometimes in separation, we seek,
To learn what love bespeaks,
To find that love transcends all,
Beyond what's said or read.

In the shadows of the moonlight,
To the dawn's first golden ray,
A miracle from heaven's grace,
I felt your presence with me.

For love knows no boundaries,

No distance can it tame,
My heart is yours forever.
For in this world of endless change,
Where love and peace abide,
My heart is yours alone.

I learned to listen to my heart,
As it discerns what's right,
And what's wrong for us.
In life's bustling crowd,
It's assured,
Though your love delays,
But it'll find you.

Fallen Leaves

Endless rain poured down,
Then autumn descends,
But bare trees stand tall,
Leaves lie fallen.

Dreary weather, dreary days,
How silently they tumble down,
Disowned, dishonoured on the ground.
As they grew old, forlorn they lie,
Trampled by ramblers passing by.

Yellow leaves do hang,
Fluttering from the autumn tree.
Cold breeze or wreath of snow,
Shaking against the wind,
Are the fallen leaves,
In empty, abandoned places,
where once sweet birds sang.

Night lengthened, shortened day,
Upon the withered love,
She lies on the pillows of yellow leaves,
And try the old tunes for an hour.

But she finds the rhythm,
Chasing golden hues,
As autumn falls.
Love takes flight,
As lovers' wrinkled hands hold tight,
Taking the eternal ride,
Pride of fallen leaves,
A timeless beauty to behold.

Traffic of life

Amidst the cacophony, chaos reigns,
Through the window's pane, my gaze strains.
Stuck in the traffic's relentless hold,
Minutes slip by,
Clouds of worry, anxieties swarm.

"I feel stuck
Uneasy and messy,
What should I do?"

Then,
The signals whispered to my soul,
"Red, green or yellow?"

When life signals red,
Pause and breathe,

To fill your cup with what you need,
Choosing the change, the shifts,
The new.
As time's bound to alter,
Like signals do.

Pause in the chaos, embrace the hue,
In red's reflection, find paths anew.

O' time set to signal yellow,
As you prepare to flow,
Desire and dream,
Let aspiration gleam,
Letting go of the stream.

Yellow's hue whispers of transition's call,
Embrace the shift, to surrender all.

Fly, flow or run;
Heed the unseen,
As time signals green.
Thou will receive more,
And opportunities will bloom.

When life's control rests in hands divine,
The ultimate traffic controller's sign.
You're smoothly navigated,
Each speed breaker crossed,
Guided by His wisdom, all is embossed.

Echoes of Awakening

Underneath the starlight,
where ambition takes flight.
In the depth of dusk,
where shadows ink in,
Amidst twilight's veil,
Prevailing are whispers of dreams.

In the realm of fantasy,
where the magic reigns;
Mapping into celestial design,
Are the destinies aligned;
In the melody of streams, lurks the rhythm of
life,
Lifting the soul to serenity, resonating and alive.

Dawning on the horizon,
symphony of possibilities spins.

In the rise of the Sun, where the ray of hope
begins.
Bathed in the golden hues,
where the sky promises a new limit.
In the echoes of silence, the voice of souls
lingers;
Speaking the unspoken.

Let the mind's eye picture,
Let the thoughts flow,
Let the memories bloom,
Let the canvas colour,
Let the wings unfurl,
Let the love untwine,
Let the desire inspire,
Let freedom be liberated.

Be the beacon of bright beauty,
Shining with grace,
Guiding through the darkest tunnel.
And rediscover the real you.

A Traveller's Heart

Let us roam,
Let us explore,
With open hearts,
Venturing forth with spirit anew,
Embracing the scares.
Whether travelling solo
Or in groups.
Unfurling mysteries of places,
As we wander through time's endless spaces.

Where we travel, our heart goes with us,

In the monument of love, they fuss.
To the city of palaces, we venture bold,
Knowing cultures unknown, stories untold.
In tribal work, legacies are cast.
Through valleys, mountains and islands afar,
Sometimes snorkelling to the depths,
Exploring beautiful reefs.
Sometimes marvelling at nature,
From illuminated beaches to towering mountain
hikes.

Seven are the Wonders of the world,
Exquisite structures,
In architecture's delight,
Each unique, a timeless sight.
Round the world we wonder,
Seeking beauty veiled,
In every corner, mysteries hailed.
Yet in our quest,
We don't just see
But to find ourselves, in our world, free.

For every adventure, every new land;
Brings moments both grand and grandstand.
Great artisans are the temple grand.
In these tranquil lands, spirituality grows;
In the four dams, as serenity flows.

Relaxed, we watch nature's art,

In every leaf and in every part.
With thoughts so positive, we rise;
Excitement dancing in our eyes
To travel is to seek;
A lovelier part to play, in every moment
Along the way.

Quest for Summit Serenity

Beckoning the adventure soul,
Trekking the mountain road,
Steep and treacherous,
A beautiful vague;
She finds herself at a pinnacle,
Having climbed with a purpose.

As she takes turns,
Curving through deep and desolate roads.
Valley of wild fearless flowers,
Streams falling onto living rocks,
The cold fresh breeze of mountain wind,
Carrying the addictive aroma of coffee
plantations,
Are the sights of sheer splendour.

As she stretches out more,

Conquering the rocks,
Till the clouds cover the mountain high,
To the invisible path.
Nurturing the heights,
Inscribed on rock,
Are the veil shrouding mysteries,
Tales tall,
Unfolding stories, untold.

As she edges past,
Little up, little through, and little round;
Through the tough pine
Like the eagle soaring high.
Wandering through roads unknown,
No limitations to the limit,
Alone and unafraid.

As she reaches the summit
With grace, gratitude and glory;
To the abode of God above,
Tiny is everything below,
Too insurmountable,
To the liberation of desire,
And the pursuit of passion.

Pillow Thoughts

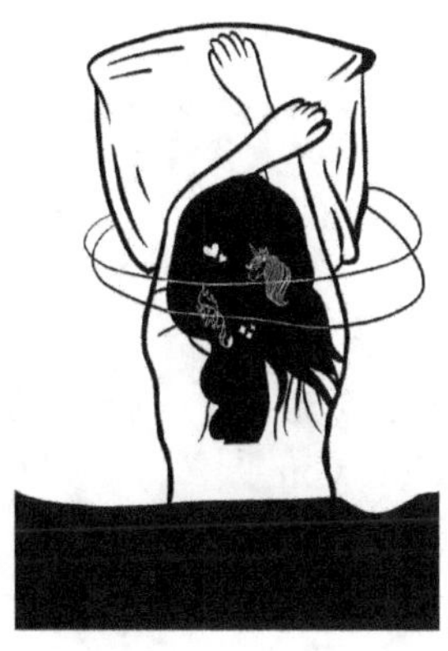

It's 5 am in the morning,
Eyes wide open,
Thoughts creeping through the night,
Wandering in flight,
Caught in sleep's plight,
Tick tock rings the alarm,
Revealing the daylight
That had already dawned.

My pillow beholding life's stride,
Sometimes absorbing tears,

Hugged tight in fear,
Alone or aloof in anxious hover.
At times smiles blush beneath its cover,
Or joyfully dance as partners.

"Yes, I am there to listen,"
As it says,
"If you can,
You can,
To master your fate."

While it preaches,
Life comes from you and not at you.
People will view you
The way you view yourself.

Moreover, it testifies,
To the storms faced with courage bright,
Turning darkest days into the light.
In every tear and every pain,
Finding the strength to rise again.

As my pillow bears witness to all I do,
And proudly declares,
"Remember when your heart was sore,
You thought you couldn't take much more?
Yet here you stand, both brave and true."

With every step, as I set the pace,

A journey lived with style and grace.
My pillow, a silent confidant,
Bearer of my dreams, woes, and wants.

The Paradox of Perfection

In pursuit of perfection, I strive;
Yet perfection remains an elusive muse.
In its endeavour, we often forgo
The raw essence of life's melody,
Wherein imperfections lie real beauty.

Every person has flaws.
Every path has bumps.
Every problem holds possibilities.
Every achievement comes with struggles.
Every rose has thorns.

With each challenge faced, you grow tall,
Like mighty oaks weathering storms,
Preaching resilience to adversities in the darkest
night.
In the journey of life, let your essence bloom,

Embrace imperfections to dispel gloom.

Let go of myths that bind you tight,
Celebrating your own imperfect light.
Chasing fleeting dreams and illusions is vain,
Instead, honour yourself and find your own
grace.

Accepting self in its entire truth,
And loving each facet in the mirror's view,
Is to believe in oneself.
As in perfection, we seek an unattainable ideal,
In imperfections, we find the beauty of what's
real.

Mapping of Life

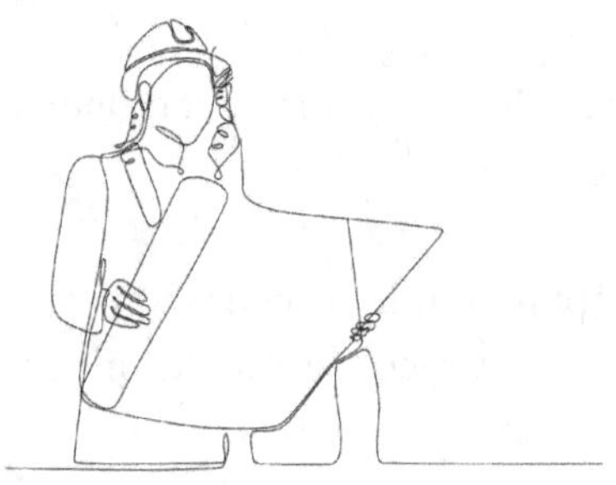

"I have to have a map!" I cry
"Even if it takes me nowhere?
I can't be without direction."

"But you are in the right direction,
Once you let yourself free, "trust me" says my
midlife soul.

The pilgrim in me travelled in darkness,
Learning to read the stars.
Letting the light of the soul shine
As I walk deeper.

In my voyage of discovery,
Seeking not new lands but seeing with new eyes,
While getting lost taught me to read the map of
life.

The architect of my life,
Exploring the path unknown,
Sailing off to the distance alone.
With God as guide, our journey unfolds,
In this invincible quest,
His hand holds firm.

Finally in the atlas of life,
Tracing my path through valleys of joy
And peaks of mountains,
Navigating through the sea
And shifting sand.

Sometimes taking the hidden road,
As there's nothing new in well-travelled paths.
But mapped in the sand, my footsteps;
That held my laughter and caught my tears.

There begins the adventure of love,
Where the map is trust,
Faith being the compass,
And friendship, our passport.
We travel to the ends of the earth for each other,
Even when we are poles apart,
Finding happiness at every destination in life.

The Closer

As I walk through the darkest tunnel,
Light seems to happen nowhere.
I'm taken aback,
As guiding ray of light strikes in,
Like magic of hope.

Got me closer
Unblocking the roads that were blocking us,
Opening up ways to reach him,
Finally, home I find through.
Blessed and lucky I feel
As the secret of magic unfolds.

Getting me closer to him,
Universe found the way,
Out of infinite intelligence,
Beautiful and best.
Gratitude fills my heart,
Dancing with joy,
Eyes brimming with tears,

As the chapter begins anew,
Ending the yearlong mysteries.

Right ends do take time.
Attracting the positivity,
Patience is what I learn,
Nevertheless,
Universe makes it happen
If it's meant to happen anyway.

Got close to him
As it rained after a hot afternoon,
Unexpected events turned good,
As they're supposed to be.
Then eyes stopped seeking
As the heart started believing.

Got me closer to him.
As time passed by,
Belief got stronger,
Love got its wings,
Unfolding myself to discover the world within.
And I fell in love with myself,
That loved him.

If You Let Me

The day I met you,
My steps stumbled in line.
Maybe cause I never knew,
what is it to be perfectly aligned?

I know you don't see yourself,
The way I look at you,
So you often argue,
When I call you special.

I think if you let me,

I will treat you like the stars in the open sky,
I'll join all insecurities,
Wrap up all your flaws,
Into a new galaxy.

All those things you can't stand
About yourself,
Are all the things
I can't go a day without.

I think if you let me,
I'll build a Belvedere,
To show you,
That just like the Polaris,
Unique as the stars of the universe,
You shine brighter.

You deserve cuddle and coffee,
In your sleepy morning and messy hair.
You deserve sweet sundaes on Sundays,
After week-long seminars on Mondays.

You deserve honesty,
In your strong determination and when you dare.
You deserve care and love,
After day-long work when you shyly smile.
You deserve to be called beautiful too,
In soft long eyelashes and deep eyes.

And if you let me,
I'll show up everyday, I promise.
While you love me, I would become your birdie,
Never let you fly away.
Until one day,
When you want,
We would fly together.

I know life isn't bright colours and fireworks,
But if you let me hold your hand,
Let me be with you,
All I want is to know you more,
Through the best and worst of what is to come,
Better than anyone else.

Crossroads

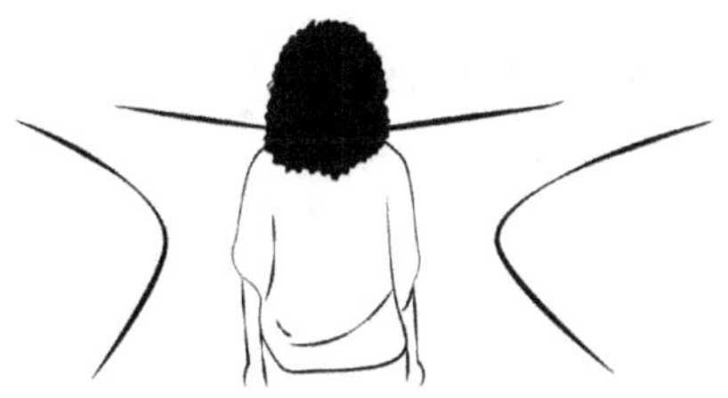

A choice
Shall I cross the sea
Or follow the stream
May be both
Or let it be.

To East rises the Sun,
To West it sets,
To the woods I travelled.
Again two roads diverged,
One with less travelled,
Caught my eyes
As my heart followed thy.

I doubted,
If the roads meet again
Or will travel parallel.

At this crossroads,
What's harder,
Holding on or letting go?

But with sighs of relief,
The choice I made,
I believed.

As You look back,
You find a reason.
As You look forward,
You know to trust.

Whether we are wrong,
Or we're right,
Wonders happen as we learn and grow.

Leap of faith

What if you were granted the power to weave
manifesting desires in thoughts you believe?
What if one act of kindness shown, has the
potential to turn a life around, and compassion
grows?
What if you replaced pessimism with optimism?
What if everything falls into place, in its own
way, even if nothing seems right today?

What if the struggles you endure, day by day,
lead you to a chapter where dreams hold sway?
What if destiny's hand leads you to one you
Love, finding solace and joy?
What if the patience you hold dear, proves
worthier than letting go, in fear?
What if passion finds your stride, unleashing
potential nowhere to hide?

What if your dedication at work takes you far?
What if dreams surpassed, beyond compare,

More than you imagined, beyond the glare?
What if that perseverance against the shadow of
doubt draws lasting achievements?

What if who you become is who you have
needed all along?
What if you laugh through the tears and dispel
your fears?
What if in every question, your answer lies?
What if impossible seems to happen anyway?

Would you change your thoughts and trust?
Would you dare to dream and find in each "what
if," an endless stream?
Would you confide in Love, rejoicing hand in
glove?
Would you open your heart to possibilities,
creating a story that imparts?

Would you stand tall, embracing life's rise and
fall?
Would you surrender the outcome, let it flow,
Release the control, let the universe show?
Would you let the treasure you hold in your
hand,
Reveal the true magnificence awaiting?
You believe so,
And that would make all the difference.

It Rained

Climbing the mountain high,
A storm brews deep inside,
Gazing at the bright blue sky,
She wished, "If only it rained..."
Stepping down in despair,
Her heart weighed in silent pain.

A lone drop kissed her cheeks,
She looked up to see the miracle of heaven,
As dark clouds engulfed the sky,
It rained.

No umbrella,
No shelter,
Or the lullabies of childhood
"Rain, rain go away."
None mattered.

Swinging to the music of rainfall,
Felt his essence in the rain's embrace,
Tears mingled with falling drops,
As joy filled her,
She smiled,
Thanking God for the beautiful trance.

No tea, no pakoda,
But ice cream's delight,
Date night in the rain, a sweet respite.
Like the scent post-rain,
Rose petals with dew,
Romancing rain,
Harvesting happiness anew.

In a season dry and still,
Enthralled by divine unfold,
She twirled
And hugged tight in delight.
Drenched in love,
Celebrating the symphony,
As the frog croaked and leaped,
It rained more.

Love, Hope and Magic

Amongst the billions,
Varied are the faces, myriad souls;
Such is the diversity of love,
So too are its seasons,
And its countless shades.

When love strikes,
I know it's magic.
When love hurts,
I know it's hard.

When mind goes against the heart,
I know what it's like.
As if you are crushed under the stone,
As if today will not end,
As if tomorrow will not come.

But I swear,
Love is power undeciphered.
If it's a storm,
The days of spring will come.
If it's black,
Colour it with red,
Creating purple hearts forever.

Love unrequited never decreases your capacity
to love.
Love aching never borrows your beautiful smile.
Loving love doesn't mean your self-love is
solitude.
Promises broken never break a kind heart.

Love may be diverted in a stormy wind.
Carry your intuition,
To strengthen your roots, trusting love.

Because what's yours will be conspired
To reach you.
So go with the flow,
Taking a step at a time,

Smiling as you believe,
As what you seek is already seeking you.

95

Racing Thoughts

Thoughts racing wildly in pavilion huge
For hopes and expectations,
Chasing dreams in endless pursuit.
In moments of loneliness,
In times of love,
In quest for success,
And for the allure of wealth,
Drowning in the debt of desires.

Then in clouds of doubt and jealousy
To the plight of pessimism,
We run and run,
Day and night
A race not for betterment
But an endless fight of comparison.

In the race of time,
We often forget,

To slow our pace and simply sit,
No!! Not to Halt,
But to observe
The story crafted with every curve,
By the Greatest Script Writer's hand.

Dreams designed with grand blueprints,
Conspiring through belief,
I dance and sway
With popcorns and fruits
And much more.
Such is the abundance of Abode;
Grateful for guidance,
As the lines of palm unfold,
Herein lies the best story
Forever planned.

The Alchemy of Universe

In the alchemy of universe,
As destiny conspires, paths align,
And dreams pursued.
Catalysts for the impossible,
Unveiled through undeniable powers within.

For the time and space entwined
In the eternal garden,
Black hole sing their silent song,
And metals turn to gold.

From that moment on,
Your thoughts owned,
Your actions indeed,
Your beliefs blend,
And shapes the reality,
In the cosmic design of stardust,

Where the universe conspires to achieve,
What the heart truly desires.

Then in the world of infinite possibilities,
You live by passion,
As sleep eludes,
Eyes awaken to dreams,
Heart gets fulfilled with possibilities anew.

In the realm unseen,
You're more than just what you are.
In search of purpose, zeroed down we roam,
Beyond what's seen is where our eyes seek.

A Sixer or Out

To be someone's first love is great,
But to be their last is beyond perfect fate.

This time it's red soil pitch,
As the skipper of the match
I heed the call.

Backed by strategies of the universe's hand,
Given full freedom to take my stride.
That's when you deliver the best.

A half year gone like whisper's fade,
Half was the experience,
Uncapped, still untested.
You don't fail, until you give up again,
For in perseverance, our strength lies,
As we chase dreams 'neath endless skies.

In the quest for the century,
Tactics were more of intuition,
As love follows no rule.
Breaking news grounds,
where heart roams free,
In love's playground.

First ball goes wide,
As he entered the field,
Gone all out with his smile.
An all-rounder, He is.

But the game is on,
Till overs are over.
Looking straight into his eyes,
Backing up for the shot,
Risking a runout.
Finally pitching the ball of my feelings,
Proposing a sixer.

Numb to the resounding cheer,
"A sixer or out?"

Maybe, it's a no-ball,
Awaiting Umpire's final call.

In the magic of moments,
We stood enthralled,
Vowed to the silence,
His voice, gently echoed,
Softly called my heart,
Claiming love's victory,
In the Finals of forever journey.

Like the Red wine!!

On the eve of Valentine's,
Like the red wine,
High on forever mine,
Before the vows,
It's our first date night.

Love in the glass of wine,
Hand in hand,
We step onto the night,
Wrapped in each other's warmth,
Like winter's burning fire.

His heartbeat, a steady rhyme,
Echoing mine, in perfect time.

A table for two,
And a glass of red wine.
With each sip shared,
A moment found,
Intoxicated by love's profound.

Underneath the moon's soft light,
In each other's arms, feeling right.
As romantic soft music serenades the air,
We sway in rhythm.

Lips intertwine, senses incredible;
In the smell of breath,
Inhaling the essence, unforgettable.
A sweet surrender,
As passion flows, fierce and tender.
Like the red wine,
A craving deep.

In love's embrace, addictive allure,
We laugh, we cry, our hearts endure.
Dopamine dances in happiness,
Reaffirming it on every date,
In love's estate.

The Sunflower and Butterflies

Graceful,
But gentle and fragile,
Got out of the cocoon,
To fly high.
Coloured bright and striped,
Beautiful as the sky,
Are the butterflies as they fly.

Frolic in the meadows
Upon the daffodils,

I chased to hold her.
She flew, full of power;
Flapping in sunshine,
Fleeting plays of colour,
I chased again,
She flew on again.

In despair, I sat down,
In fields where golden dreams do sway,
Sunflower turned to me,
Its petals sunkissed array
In the hues of gold,
It laid the way.

As more sunflowers, I plant with care,
The butterflies flew from far away.
They perch not just on petals bright,
But also on my hand, a wondrous sight.

In the garden of love and loyalty
I dance to express deep love
And admiration.

In the nature's unique creation,
Delving into the marvellous world of magic.
As butterflies grace the sunflower's bloom,
I beckon love, dispelling gloom.

Witness to Love

Why do we marry?
Is it the shadow of loneliness?
Or the curls of culture.

Amid a billion souls in this beautiful world,
Two unknown wandering hearts,
Found and chose each other
In a commitment for lifetime,
Captures God's miraculous creation.

A promise to care, unwavering.

In moments of laughter,
In tears that may fall,
But find strength in faith,
Rising from the call.

You learn to love everything about that person,
Admiring good things,
To accepting bad things,
Sometimes embracing all that can be terrible,
And excitement over mundane things.

All of it,
All the time,
Each and everyday.
A promise that,
Your life won't go unseen,
For I am here, noticing.
Your life won't go unwitnessed,
For I will be your witness.

It's of the heart,
And the heart is the chalice of love.
The vows to cherish, love, and honour,
Radiating peace, goodwill, and warmth.

Sometimes nagging, yet affectionate,
Sometimes faults, yet forgiven.
Sometimes sorrows, yet celebrate together,
A companion to all that comes and goes.

With each gentle touch, with every shared
glance,
Dancing to the rhythm of love's sweet trance.
Bound not just by words, but by hearts' decree,
Love is what love does,
In marriage, they become much more.
And there, our souls united, forevermore.

Walk to Remember

One step,
Two, then thousands,
A long Journey of life,
It wasn't September,
Neither was it November.

Nostalgia of the first walk,
As we walk through life,
Just walking,
Forward to the unknown,

We keep walking without a turn.

On the way,
As the moon was shiny,
Two of a kind on a walk to remember,
We didn't know where to go,
Days came, night followed,
Hot or rainy weather,
Then came spring of hope,
Many days within the month,
Walking somewhere,
Where promising,
Call it our destiny.

A walk to remember,
Down the aisle I tread,
With the man who gave me life,
To the man who loves me true,
To the promises of growing old together,
In our hearts, always new.

We just keep walking,
Walks of life,
Forget not to forever smile,
With blessings divine,
A walk to remember for life.

Winter under Northern lights

In the blanket of stars,
Beneath the heart of winter's silent night,
And snow-clad trees,
Whispers carried on an icy breeze.

Under the moon's soft ethereal glow,
As two souls wander,
Meandering hand in hand,
Through fields of dream.

Yet in the cold, warmth resides,

In the arms of each other.
Also in heated breath, on numbing lips,
As they lay under the naked tree,
The frost rest on the face,
Sparkling to the angelic sight.

The northern lights,
A myriad of colours,
Painted the winter sky,
Our stories that hadn't been heard yet.

As the shimmering eyes,
Let the colour wash to paint
His dreams and happiness
With her now.
As he covers her in his warmth.
And built the igloo of love,
Far from complexities and chaos.

An Ode to Time

Tick tock tick
As time passing by,
I lay under the darkness of the sky,
In the silence of the night.
Contemplating the hand, wielding power;
As it moves, ticking every second.

Time is timeless in our hands it lies,
There is none to count our time.
What is our life, full of care,
If we have no time to stand and stare.

Time passing by,
I lay down to feel all the time in the world.

Time is precious,
When we respect the present.
Time is priceless,
When we give it to our loved ones.
Time is patience,
When we are resilient while awaiting the right
time.
Time is blessing,
When we are kind.
Time is now,
To change the world within.

Let the time take its natural course.
As it knows no divide,
Impartial to all,
The great equaliser.
In the river of moments, it flows;
Each second a story, each heartbeat it knows.
With every tick of the clock, it marches on,
A silent witness to all that comes and goes.

There is time for everything.
Grace each moment with joy, love and laughter
as time passes,
For these are the treasures of our past.

Moreover the time is not fleeting,
But a timeless art,
With an eternal rhythm,
Stitched in every heart.

Footprints of Soul Unique

Millions of faces, each one is unique,
Thoughts are diverge,
But no second repeat,
No second version,
Nor can you create,
Each soul, a tale;
Alive and innate.

A story unique to yours,
In rain's embrace or sunny glow,
Or life's ebb and flow, a constant show.

From days of sorrow to joy untold,

In every journey, stories unfold.
As doomed days fade, bright ones arise,
Change is the law under azure skies.

Through winding roads, you find your way,
To vistas fair, where dreams hold sway.

In zigzag lines, a story flows,
Of joys, of pains,
The highs and lows.
Dancing in rhythm
Are the waves defined,
A map of heart alive,
Until the day, the beat fades to a single line.

So do all you aspire,
Let dreams inspire,
And experiences explored.

Forget, forgive,
But keep no regrets.
For live with passion,
Marking the imprint of your soul eternal.

In your hand lies a journey grand,
Beautiful and inspiring, like shifting sand.
For generations to come, hence,
Walk the path where your footprints stand.

The Dance of Fun

In a world where laughter reigns,
Where joy flows like summer rains.
Laugh, oh laugh, with all your heart's delight,
Let your body sparkle with the radiance of light.
There's a place where worries shun,
In the merry dance of fun.

Skipping stones on crystal lakes,
Or baking cakes and sweet milkshakes,
To playing hide and seek beneath the sun,
All that is a part of endless fun.

Giggles bubbling, spirits high,
As Kites soar into the sky,
Or Splashing in the midday sun.
Oh, the ways we cherish fun.

Tickle fights and pillow forts,
To friendly games and lively sports,
Are the moments shared with everyone,
In the boundless realm of fun.

Live fully and love loudly.
Dare to hope and dream,
Flowing with falls,
As it's okay if the glass is half empty,
You can always fill it with joy.

Embracing life's journey,
Fearlessly venture forth,
With love as your guide.
For in our hearts, life's race is won,
When we bask in beams of fun.

Enjoy the wonderful nature,
To believe in the magic of existence,
'Cause each thing we see today,
Once a thought, believed.

Each moment, each second,
Precious, your beautiful smile,
So laugh, oh laugh;
'Cause you live only once.

The Woods of Gold

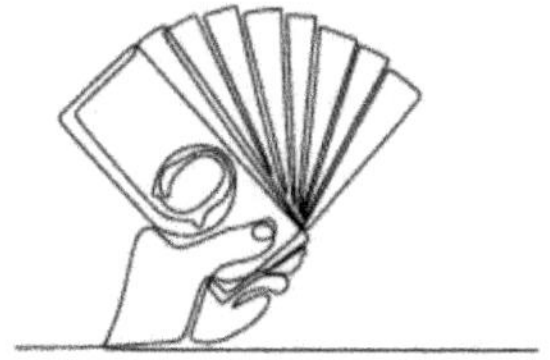

In the woods of wealth, where green bills grow,
I stumbled upon a path to and fro.
The trees stood tall, with branches of gold,
And the wind whispered secrets, untold.

Through the thicket of stocks and bonds, I
roamed,
In search of riches, to build a home.
But as I journeyed, my heart grew weary,
For amidst the wealth, I found little cheer.

For money, like ivy, can strangle and bind,
Leaving the soul barren, empty of mind.
In the pursuit of fortune, we often lose sight,
Of the simple joys, in morning's light.

So I turned away from the woods of gold,
To find true wealth, in stories untold.
For in laughter shared and love's embrace,
Lies a treasure no riches can replace.

Pink or Blue?

"Who am I?"
Caught in between the urge to hide,
And wanting to be seen.
Is my worth in dollars earned?
Or in the best of hundred clicks,
Or the followers and likes.
Because showing others,
To be accepted,
Is unsettling with self.

"Pink or blue?"
It has taken me a blue moon,
To figure out,
And write something beautiful,
About myself,
All things I like or dislike.

My actual choices and my true delight,
My passion deep,
My happiness, found.

No one can make me feel loved
Unless I love myself.
When I untethered everything
That showed not me,
I realised my abundance is priceless
And not quantifiable.
Pink or blue, the shades of me;
To cherish all that I can be.

The Mirror's Tale

I am you, I mirror you in reflection.
I am the beauty you behold that shines anew.
I am the eyes that sparkle with dreams untold.
I am the lips that smile through ups and downs.
I am the face that tells tales of joy and sorrow.
I am the lines etched deeper in the palm every
tomorrow.

I am as you see me,
I mirror your inner power.
I am the courage when you need strength.

I am the portrayal of confidence when you have
the world to confront.
I am the echo of memories and moments.
I am the intuition that guides your heart to a
symphony.
I am your voice amidst the chaos outside.

I am as you look at me.
I am the clarity that envisions in ripples of water.
I am the guiding light from the lighthouse as
waves hit hard.
I am your dark shadow at dusk, till dawn brings
new beginnings.
I am the hidden treasure shimmering in the
moon's gentle light.

I see you more than what you are,
A journey of self-discovery, wild and free.
I am your reflection where truth never lies.
I am the transformation,
As you evolve and grow.
I am the kindred grace, a reminder of beauty in
every embrace.
I am the flaws and virtues of you intertwine,
As in the mirror of self, a story traced.

I am you, with reflected appraisal.
I am the sketch of your scars and struggles
penned.

Yet towards bright endings and resilience you
lend.
I am the lens capturing the pursuit of the real
you.
I am the canvas you painted with hues.
I am the reflection of your eternal soul that took
the shape of beautiful you.
I am you, your best version shining through.

A love Letter To Me from Me

As the star shining in the dark starry sky,
You came in with a rich, beautiful smile,
Sparkling eyes that could beguile,
A soft voice that calmed the wild,
I fell for you, just like a lover.

Your simplicity caught my heart,
In a world complex, you are an art.
Unique you are, with a gift so rare,
You see possibilities where others despair.

In every moment, you seek to grow,
To be the best that you can show.
Through ups and downs,
A shining light and guiding star.
Exploring life with eager eyes,
A better version, always on the rise.

You forgive and forgave,
For future stakes.
You foster positivity,
Through compassion and care.
Each choice, each path, has brought you here,
To a place that's filled with love, not fear.

Lovable when you're around the kids,
A tender heart beneath the lids.
Innocence shines where pure joy lives,
And growing friendship confides.
Like water, you blend and flow,
With every age, you easily go.

Nerdy charm embracing dreams,
Through all these traits, I see the light,
A soul that's bold, courage bright.
A heart that loves before all else,
Not just for you, but for love itself.

You look sexy in your shy disguise,
Crazy adventures in your eyes.

Daring spirit, brave and true,
In every way, I fell for you.

So here's to you, with love so deep,
A bond that's ours alone to keep.
With every word, this truth I send,
You are at your own best, truest love.

Spring of Hope

In the spring of hope,
Buds grow,
Whispers of promise,
Into every flower.
Petals dance with the breeze's embrace,
As dreams awaken, in nature's grace.

In fields of green,
The skies are so blue.
From barren branches,
Life bursts forth,

And hope blossoms bright.
From the depths of the earth to the heights
above,
Reveals this season,
A symphony of life,
Singing of love.

With each dawn,
A chance to believe,
In the magic of what we can achieve.
For in the spring of hope,
Hearts align,
And possibilities bloom.

In the garden of optimism,
We joyfully roam,
For in the spring of hope,
We found our home.

So let us cherish the season,
Spreading sweet fragrance of love,
And let our spirits rise.
For in the spring of hope,
May we find our way,
To brighter tomorrows,
Come what may.

The Gratitude

From the womb of my mother
The journey begins.
You guided me in your soul's light,
Through the steps I struggled,
You held my palms tight.
Every emotion I felt, misaligned;
You gave strength to fight.
When things got messed up,
You made it right.

To every purpose I believed,

You gave the flight.
In the darkest night
When fear took height,
You unlocked doors
To the opportunities bright.

You taught me to think, act and believe.
Took away all my grief,
To give a sigh of relief.
Affirmed positive thoughts,
To attain dreams seemingly impossible
From the quantum of infinite possibilities.

Patience is what I seek,
In times when I freak.
And courage to reach the finishing line,
When attempts fail to align.
You are the connection I find
To the peaceful calm mind.
Being a protective barrier
You make me smile happier.

You are the power of healing stone
To the remedies unknown.
A beautiful sight of magic,
Where miracle is charismatic;
A blessing in disguise,
To receive more than desired prize.

Love is power
And Faith is surrender,
In the Abundance of universe,
Grateful to You
For life, so precious per se.